The
Wiersbe
BIBLE STUDY SERIES

The **Wiersbe**
BIBLE STUDY SERIES

ROMANS

How to Be

Right with

God, Yourself,

and Others

transforming lives together

THE WIERSBE BIBLE STUDY SERIES: ROMANS
Published by David C. Cook
4050 Lee Vance View
Colorado Springs, CO 80918 U.S.A.

David C. Cook Distribution Canada
55 Woodslee Avenue, Paris, Ontario, Canada N3L 3E5

David C. Cook U.K., Kingsway Communications
Eastbourne, East Sussex BN23 6NT, England

David C. Cook and the graphic circle C logo
are registered trademarks of Cook Communications Ministries.

All Scripture quotations in this study are taken from the *Holy Bible, New International
Version*®. *NIV*®. Copyright © 1973, 1978, 1984 by International Bible Society.
Used by permission of Zondervan. All rights reserved.

In the *Be Right* excerpts, all Scripture quotations, unless otherwise noted,
are taken from the King James Version of the Bible. (Public Domain.)
All excerpts taken from *Be Right,* second edition,
published by David C. Cook in 2008
© 1977 Warren W. Wiersbe, ISBN 978-1-4347-6847-6

ISBN 978-0-7814-4572-6

© 2008 Warren W. Wiersbe

The Team: Steve Parolini, Gudmund Lee, Amy Kiechlin,
Jack Campbell, and Susan Vannaman
Series Cover Design: John Hamilton Design
Cover Photo: iStockPhoto

Printed in the United States of America
First Edition 2008

3 4 5 6 7 8 9 10

102108

Contents

Introduction to Romans

Righteousness Revealed

If you're tired of all the wrong things in your life, in the lives of others, and in this world, then Paul's epistle to the Romans is the book for you.

The theme of Romans is "the righteousness of God." In this letter, Paul tells how to Be Right—with God, ourselves, and others. Paul also explains how one day God will make creation right, and even solve "the Jewish problem" and bring peace on earth.

Romans was not written for woolgatherers or religious scholars. You will have to think as you study this letter, but the rewards will be worth the effort. If you understand Romans, you'll have the key to understanding the rest of the Bible and the secret to successful Christian living.

A Book of Great Influence

On May 24, 1738, a discouraged missionary went "very unwillingly" to a religious meeting in London. There, a miracle took place. "About a quarter before nine," he wrote in his journal, "I felt my heart strangely warmed. I felt I did trust in Christ, Christ alone, for salvation; and an assurance was given me that He had taken away my sins, even mine, and saved me from the law of sin and death."

That missionary was John Wesley. The message he heard that evening was the preface to Martin Luther's commentary on Romans.

The Protestant Reformation and the Wesleyan Revival were both the fruit of this wonderful letter written by Paul from Corinth around the year AD 56.

Imagine! You and I can read and study the same inspired letter that brought life and power to Luther and Wesley! And the same Holy Spirit who taught them can teach us! You and I can experience revival in our hearts, homes, and churches if the message of this letter grips us as it has gripped men and women of faith in centuries past.

—Warren W. Wiersbe

How to Use This Study

This study is designed for both individual and small-group use. We've divided it into twelve lessons—each references one or more chapters in Warren W. Wiersbe's commentary *Be Right* (second edition, David C. Cook, 2008). While reading *Be Right* is not a prerequisite for going through this study, the additional insights and background Wiersbe offers can greatly enhance your study experience.

The **Getting Started** questions at the beginning of each lesson offer you an opportunity to record your first thoughts and reactions to the study text. This is an important step in the study process as those "first impressions" often include clues about what it is your heart is longing to discover.

The bulk of the study is found in the **Going Deeper** questions. These dive into the Bible text and, along with helpful excerpts from Wiersbe's commentary, help you examine not only the original context and meaning of the verses but also modern application.

Looking Inward narrows the focus down to your personal story. These intimate questions can be a bit uncomfortable at times, but don't shy away from honesty here. This is where you are asked to stand before the mirror of God's Word and look closely at what you see. It's the place to take a good look at yourself in light of the lesson and search for ways in which you can grow in faith.

Going Forward is the place where you can commit to paper those things you want or need to do in order to better live out the discoveries you made in the "Looking Inward" section. Don't skip or skim through this. Take the time to really consider what practical steps you might take to move closer to Christ. Then share your thoughts with a trusted friend who can act as an encourager and accountability partner.

Finally, there is a brief **Seeking Help** section to close the lesson. This is a reminder for you to invite God into your spiritual-growth process. If you choose to write out a prayer in this section, come back to it as you work through the lesson and continue to seek the Holy Spirit's guidance as you discover God's will for your life.

Tips for Small Groups

A small group is a dynamic thing. One week it might seem like a group of close-knit friends. The next it might seem more like a group of uncomfortable strangers. A small-group leader's role is to read these subtle changes and adjust the tone of the discussion accordingly.

Small groups need to be safe places for people to talk openly. It is through shared wrestling with difficult life issues that some of the greatest personal growth is discovered. But in order for the group to feel safe, participants need to know it's okay *not* to share sometimes. Always invite honest disclosure, but never force someone to speak if he or she isn't comfortable doing so. (A savvy leader will follow up later with a group member who isn't comfortable sharing in a group setting to see if a one-on-one discussion is more appropriate.)

Have volunteers take turns reading excerpts from Scripture or from the commentary. The more each person is involved even in the mundane tasks, the more he or she will feel comfortable opening up in more meaningful ways.

Finally, soak your group meetings in prayer—before you begin, during as needed, and always at the end of your time together.

Life-Changing Letter
(ROMANS 1:1–17)

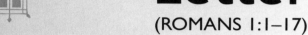

Before you begin ...
- *Pray for the Holy Spirit to reveal truth and wisdom as you go through this lesson.*
- *Read Romans 1:1–17. This lesson references chapter 1 in* Be Right. *It will be helpful for you to have your Bible and a copy of the commentary available as you work through this lesson.*

Getting Started

From the Commentary

Paul's epistle to the Romans is still transforming people's lives, just the way it transformed Martin Luther and John Wesley. The one Scripture above all others that brought Luther out of mere religion into the joy of salvation by grace, through faith, was Romans 1:17: "The just shall live by faith."

—*Be Right,* page 17

1. As you read this first passage from Romans, what emotions do you detect in Paul's "voice"? What is the overall purpose of this introduction?

More to Consider: This letter had a powerful impact on well-known influencers of the church such as Martin Luther and John Wesley. What clues about the importance of this letter to the early church do you discover in the opening verses?

2. Choose one verse or phrase from Romans 1:1–17 that stands out to you. This could be something you're intrigued by, something that makes you uncomfortable, something that puzzles you, something that resonates with you, or just something you want to examine further. Write that here. What strikes you about this verse?

Going Deeper
From the Commentary

The word Paul used for *servant* would be meaningful to the Romans, because it is the word *slave*. There were an estimated sixty million slaves in the Roman Empire, and a slave was looked on as a piece of property, not a person.

> In loving devotion, Paul had enslaved himself to Christ, to
> be His servant and obey His will.
>
> —*Be Right*, page 18

3. What comes to mind when you read the word *servant*? How easy or difficult is it for Christians today to understand the implications of Paul's use of this word for *slave*? What does it mean to be "enslaved to Christ" in today's world?

From the Commentary

> When he was a Jewish rabbi, Paul was separated as a Pharisee to the laws and traditions of the Jews. But when he yielded to Christ, he was separated to the gospel and its ministry. *Gospel* means "the good news." ...
>
> The gospel is not a new message; it was promised in the Old Testament, beginning in Genesis 3:15. The prophet Isaiah certainly preached the gospel in passages such as Isaiah 1:18 and chapters 53 and 55.
>
> —*Be Right*, page 19

4. Take a moment to read Genesis 3:15 and Isaiah 1:18 (and skim chapters 53 and 55). How is the gospel message presented in these passages? In what ways is it presented as "good news"?

From the History Books

If you scroll back to the beginning of the Protestant Reformation in 1517, you'll discover Martin Luther's challenges to the practices of the Roman Catholic Church: his "Ninety-Five Theses on the Power of Indulgences." Luther's discontent with this practice (and others) ultimately led to a fracturing of Christianity and the growth of Protestantism. Key to Luther's argument was the idea that Scripture should be the sole measure of theology. The book of Romans is central to this "sola scriptura" approach since it contains some of the most significant theological content.

5. What do you think the church would look like today without the efforts of Reformers like Luther? What is significant about Luther's belief that Scripture alone should give us our theology? How do we uncover theology from Scripture? What are the challenges we face when trying to understand theology from Scripture? The risks of counting on extrabiblical sources?

From the Commentary

> Paul's special commission was to take the gospel to the Gentiles (the word *nations* means Gentiles), and this is why he was planning to go to Rome, the very capital of the empire. He was a preacher of the gospel, and the gospel was for all nations. In fact, Paul was anxious to go to Spain with the message of Christ (Rom. 15:28).
>
> —*Be Right*, page 20

6. In what ways does Paul's excitement about preaching the gospel to the nations inspire you? In what ways does it intimidate you? How are the challenges Paul faced in presenting the gospel like or unlike the challenges faced by the church today?

From the Commentary

> What a testimony: "I am a debtor! I am eager! I am not ashamed!" Why would Paul even be tempted to be ashamed of the gospel as he contemplated his trip to Rome? For one thing, the gospel was identified with a poor Jewish carpenter who was crucified. The Romans had no special appreciation for the Jews, and crucifixion was the lowest form of execution given a criminal. Why put your faith in a Jew who was crucified?
>
> —*Be Right*, page 23

7. Consider Wiersbe's question in the excerpt: Why would Paul be tempted to be ashamed of the gospel? How is this like or unlike the way Christians today feel about sharing the gospel? How does someone move from being "ashamed" to being "eager" to share the gospel?

From the Commentary

> Power is the one thing that Rome boasted of the most.
> Greece might have its philosophy, but Rome had its
> power. The fear of Rome hovered over the empire like a
> cloud. Were they not the conquerors? Were not the
> Roman legions stationed all over the known world? But
> with all of her military power, Rome was still a weak
> nation. The philosopher Seneca called the city of Rome
> "a cesspool of iniquity"; and the writer Juvenal called it a
> "filthy sewer into which the dregs of the empire flood."
>
> No wonder Paul was not ashamed: He was taking to sin-
> ful Rome the one message that had the power to change
> people's lives!
>
> —*Be Right*, page 24

8. What is a modern comparison to Rome and its power? In what ways is today's church called to respond to the very same sort of need that Paul saw in Rome?

More to Consider: Think about some of the "Romes" you have encoun-
tered in your life (communities or individuals in dire need of a Sav-
ior). What are some ways your church is reaching out to these people?
Is the church "eager" as Paul was? Why or why not?

From the Commentary

> God does not ask people to *behave* in order to be saved,
> but to *believe*. It is faith in Christ that saves the sinner.
> Eternal life in Christ is one gift that is suitable for all
> people, no matter what their need may be or what their
> station in life.
>
> —*Be Right*, page 25

9. Respond to Wiersbe's comment: "God does not ask men to behave, but
to believe." How does faith save the sinner? If eternal life in Christ is a gift
suitable for all people, what does that compel us as Christians to do when
we meet others who do not know Christ?

From the Commentary

> When you study Romans, you walk into a courtroom.
> First, Paul called Jews and Gentiles to the stand and
> found both guilty before God. Then he explained God's
> marvelous way of salvation—justification by faith. At this
> point, he answered his accusers and defended God's sal-
> vation. "This plan of salvation will encourage people to
> sin!" they cry. "It is against the very law of God!" But Paul

refuted them, and in so doing explained how the Christian can experience victory, liberty, and security.

—*Be Right*, page 26

10. Paul speaks to both the Jews and Gentiles in Romans. Why is this important to the theology of the gospel? What does it say about God's grace? Why do you think accusers believed Paul's explanation of the plan of salvation would encourage people to sin?

Looking Inward

Take a moment to reflect on all that you've explored thus far in this study of Romans 1:1–17. Review your notes and answers and think about how each of these things matters in your life today.

> *Tips for Small Groups: To get the most out of this section, form pairs or trios and have group members take turns answering these questions. Be honest and as open as you can in this discussion, but most of all, be encouraging and supportive of others. Be sensitive to those who are going through particularly difficult times and don't press for people to speak if they're uncomfortable doing so.*

11. In what ways are you inspired by Paul's opening to Romans? What are some of the things you're most thankful for in your faith journey?

12. Are you bold like Paul in your "missionary journeys" of life? Why or why not? What is it about Paul's approach to spreading the gospel that intimidates you most?

13. Can Christians be ashamed of the gospel? Why or why not? What would that look like? In what ways are you eager to spread the gospel? How do you deal with the insecurities that sometimes accompany a desire to share the good news? What does it look like to trust God's power in this?

Going Forward

14. Think of one or two things that you have learned that you'd like to work on in the coming week. Remember that this is all about quality, not quantity. It's better to work on one specific area of life and do it well than to work on many and do poorly (or to be so overwhelmed that you simply don't try).

Do you need to show your thanks for all those who have helped you in your walk of faith? Do you need to dig deeper into Scripture to understand the theology of salvation? Do you need to learn boldness? Be specific. Go back through Romans 1:1–17 and put a star next to the phrase or verse that is most encouraging to you. Consider memorizing this verse.

Real-Life Application Ideas: Practice being unashamed about the gospel by sharing your faith story in an appropriate venue (perhaps at lunch with close nonbeliever friends, or even among strangers if you're unafraid to engage them about God's work in your life). Afterward, share with a close friend what the experience was like and what you've learned from it to better prepare you the next time you are called or led to stand up for what you believe.

Seeking Help

15. Write a prayer below (or simply pray one in silence), inviting God to work on your mind and heart in those areas you've previously noted. Be honest about your desires and fears.

Notes for Small Groups:
- *Look for ways to put into practice the things you wrote in the "Going Forward" section in this lesson. Talk with other group members about your ideas and commit to being accountable to one another.*
- *During the coming week, ask the Holy Spirit to continue to reveal truth to you from what you've read and studied.*
- *Before you start the next lesson, read Romans 1:18— 3:20. For more in-depth lesson preparation, read chapter 2, "When God Gives Up," in* Be Right.

Guilty!
(ROMANS 1:18—3:20)

Before you begin …
- *Pray for the Holy Spirit to reveal truth and wisdom as you go through this lesson.*
- *Read Romans 1:18—3:20. This lesson references chapter 2 in* Be Right. *It will be helpful for you to have your Bible and a copy of the commentary available as you work through this lesson.*

Getting Started

From the Commentary

"Hear ye! Hear ye! Court is now in session!" Paul could have used those awesome words at this point in his letter, because Romans 1:18 is the door that leads us into God's courtroom. The theme of Romans is the righteousness of God, but Paul had to begin with the unrighteousness of humankind. Until person knows he is a sinner, he cannot appreciate the gracious salvation God offers in Jesus Christ.

—*Be Right,* page 31

1. What is the first thing that comes to mind when you read this passage? How are all men and women guilty before God?

More to Consider: What does the word righteousness *mean? What do you think it means to a nonbeliever? Why does being "right before God" matter to our faith?*

2. Choose one verse or phrase from Romans 1:18—3:20 that stands out to you. This could be something you're intrigued by, something that makes you uncomfortable, something that puzzles you, something that resonates with you, or just something you want to examine further. Write that here. What strikes you about this passage?

Going Deeper

From the Commentary

> Human history began with people knowing God. Human history is not the story of a beast that worshipped idols, and then evolved into a person worshipping one God.

Human history is just the opposite: People began knowing God but turned from the truth and rejected God.

—*Be Right*, page 32

3. Circle all of the things Paul writes that illustrate why man is guilty before
God. Why do you think Paul singles out "judging others" in this passage?
How is man's judgment of others evidence of rejecting God?

From the Commentary

From idolatry to immorality is just one short step. If man
is his own god, then he can do whatever he pleases and
fulfill his desires without fear of judgment.

—*Be Right*, page 33

4. What is the "one short step" between idolatry and immorality? What
does it mean that God will judge everyone according to his deeds? How
does this line up with God's righteousness? How about with what it means
to be made righteous by God?

From Today's World

Review any popular magazine, Web site, or television show, and you'll quickly see that today's world is rife with "idol worship." One of the more popular television programs of today boldly proclaims this "idol-ness" in its very title. But many of today's idols are not quite so easily identified.

5. Why is our culture so obsessed with "idols"? Though we may use the term *idol* flippantly or without regard to the biblical definition of the word, the truth of our desire to celebrate people, places, and things as idols remains strong. What are the dangers of playing "fast and loose" with these idols?

From the Commentary

Men not only committed these sins in open defiance of God, but encouraged others and applauded them when they sinned. How far man fell! He began glorifying God but ended exchanging that glory for idols. He began knowing God but ended refusing to keep the knowledge of God in his mind and heart. He began as the highest of God's creatures, made in the image of God, but he ended lower than the beasts and insects, because he worshipped them as his gods. The verdict? "They are without excuse" (Rom. 1:20).

—*Be Right*, page 34

6. What are some evidences that man was once the "highest of God's creatures"? Why are we "without excuse" when it comes to our sins? Are all sins committed in open defiance of God? Explain. How do people today exchange God's glory for idols?

More to Consider: Romans 1:26 states that God permitted people to go on in their sins and reap the consequences. Why didn't God just step in and save everyone from his or her sins? What role does God's allowance of man to continue in sin play in the theology of salvation?

From the Commentary

God's judgment is according to truth. He does not have one standard for the Jews and another for the Gentiles. One who reads the list of sins in Romans 1:29–32 cannot escape the fact that each person is guilty of at least one of them. There are "sins of the flesh and of the spirit" (2 Cor. 7:1); there are "prodigal sons" and "elder brothers" (Luke 15:11–32). When they condemned the Gentiles for their sins, the Jews were really condemning themselves. As the old saying puts it, "When you point your finger at somebody else, the other three are pointing at you."

—*Be Right*, pages 35–36

7. Review the list of sins in Romans 1:29–32. How does this list prove all of mankind is sinful? What is the difference between sins of the flesh and sins of the spirit?

From the Commentary

> In Romans 2:6–11, Paul was not teaching salvation by character or good deeds. He was explaining another basic principle of God's judgment: God judges according to deeds, just as He judges according to truth. Paul was dealing here with the consistent actions of a person's life, the total impact of his character and conduct. For example, David committed some terrible sins, but the total emphasis of his life was obedience to God. Judas confessed his sin and supplied the money for buying a cemetery for strangers, yet the total emphasis of his life was disobedience and unbelief.
>
> —*Be Right*, page 36

8. Why is it important to note that God judges according to deeds *and* truth? What is your reaction to Wiersbe's explanation of David's "total emphasis" of his life? His explanation of Judas's "total emphasis"? Does the church judge according to the "total emphasis" or individual sins? What does this tell you about the role of the church versus God's role in the lives of sinners?

From the Commentary

> God judges according to "the secrets of men" (Rom. 2:16),
> so that He is not impressed with mere outward formalities.
>
> —*Be Right*, page 38

9. What are some examples of "outward formalities" that man might choose to judge others by? What are the "secrets of the heart" Paul is referring to here?

From the Commentary

> The word *therefore* in Romans 3:20 carries the meaning of "because," and gives the reason why the whole world is guilty. No flesh can obey God's law and be justified (declared righteous) in His sight. It is true that "the doers of the law shall be justified" (Rom. 2:13), but nobody can do what the law demands. This inability is one way that people know they are sinners. When they try to obey the law, they fail miserably and need to cry out for God's mercy. Neither Jew nor Gentile can obey God's law; therefore God must save sinners by some other means.
>
> —*Be Right*, pages 40–41

10. Circle all the times Paul writes "therefore" and "because." Why do you

think there are so many of these in Romans? What is significant about the "therefore" in 3:20?

Looking Inward

Take a moment to reflect on all that you've explored thus far in this study of Romans 1:18—3:20. Review your notes and answers and think about how each of these things matters in your life today.

> *Tips for Small Groups: To get the most out of this section, form pairs or trios and have group members take turns answering these questions. Be honest and as open as you can in this discussion, but most of all, be encouraging and supportive of others. Be sensitive to those who are going through particularly difficult times and don't press for people to speak if they're uncomfortable doing so.*

11. In what specific ways does this section of Romans speak to your story? In what ways are you "guilty as charged"? How do you respond to Paul's words? Are you humbled? Challenged? Inspired? Explain.

12. What are some of the "idols" you worship? Are there such things as "harmless" idols? Why or why not? What are some practical steps you can take to point your heart and desire toward God instead of the idols that compete for your attention?

13. What are the "secrets of your heart"? How does your heart compare to your outward expression of your faith? If there is a disconnect, what is causing that disparity? What would your outward expressions look like if they perfectly matched your heart?

Going Forward

14. Think of one or two things that you have learned that you'd like to work on in the coming week. Remember that this is all about quality, not quantity. It's better to work on one specific area of life and do it well than to work on many and do poorly (or to be so overwhelmed that you simply don't try).

Do you need to reduce the number of idols in your life? Line up your action with your heart? Be specific. Go back through Romans 1:18—3:20 and put a star next to the phrase or verse that is most encouraging to you. Consider memorizing this verse.

Real-Life Application Ideas: Compare Paul's "courtroom scene" with those portrayed on popular television shows. Talk with a friend about what it might be like to sit in the chair of the accused as if Paul were presenting this case against you. How would that play on television?

What is the main difference between Paul's courtroom drama and those acted out by Hollywood?

Seeking Help

15. Write a prayer below (or simply pray one in silence), inviting God to work on your mind and heart in those areas you've previously noted. Be honest about your desires and fears.

Notes for Small Groups:

- *Look for ways to put into practice the things you wrote in the "Going Forward" section in this lesson. Talk with other group members about your ideas and commit to being accountable to one another.*
- *During the coming week, ask the Holy Spirit to continue to reveal truth to you from what you've read and studied.*
- *Before you start the next lesson, read Romans 3:21— 4:25. For more in-depth lesson preparation, read chapter 3, "Father Abraham," in* Be Right.

Justified
(ROMANS 3:21—4:25)

Before you begin ...
- *Pray for the Holy Spirit to reveal truth and wisdom as you go through this lesson.*
- *Read Romans 3:21—4:25. This lesson references chapter 3 in* Be Right. *It will be helpful for you to have your Bible and a copy of the commentary available as you work through this lesson.*

Getting Started

From the Commentary

Paul's theme in the second section of his letter was salvation—righteousness declared. He proved that all people are sinners; so his next goal was to explain how sinners can be saved. The theological term for this salvation is *justification by faith.* Justification is the act of God whereby He declares the believing sinner righteous in Christ on the basis of the finished work of

Christ on the cross. Each part of this definition is important, so we must consider it carefully.

—*Be Right,* page 45

1. What do you think of when you hear the word *justification*? How is the common usage of the word different from Paul's use? What does it mean to be justified by faith?

More to Consider: Wiersbe writes, "Justification is an act, not a process. There are no degrees of justification." Why is it important to see justification as a single act? What implications does this have for believers? Nonbelievers?

2. Choose one verse or phrase from Romans 3:21—4:25 that stands out to you. This could be something you're intrigued by, something that makes you uncomfortable, something that puzzles you, something that resonates with you, or just something you want to examine further. Write that here. What strikes you about this verse?

Going Deeper

From the Commentary

> Do not confuse justification and sanctification. Sanctification is the process whereby God makes the believer more and more like Christ. Sanctification may change from day to day. Justification never changes. When the sinner trusts Christ, God declares him righteous, and that declaration will never be repealed. God looks on us and deals with us as though we had never sinned at all!
>
> —*Be Right*, pages 45–46

3. How might Paul's description of *justification* have led to the early Christians' concern that his theology might promote wanton sinning? If justification occurs just once, is that alone enough for a Christian? Why or why not? How do justification and sanctification work together in the life of a believer?

From the Commentary

> Under the Old Testament law, righteousness came by people behaving, but under the gospel, righteousness comes by believing.
>
> —*Be Right*, page 46

4. Respond to Wiersbe's comment in the excerpt. In what ways do Christians today still attempt to attain righteousness by behaving? Why is this so tempting for Christians? Is it easy or difficult to accept the truth that righteousness comes merely by believing? Explain.

From Today's World

It's a common belief in today's world that you get into heaven by being "a good person" and "doing good things." Take a moment to review the spin popular culture puts on actors' and musicians' and other public figures' "acts of goodness" (everything from driving a hybrid automobile to adopting orphans from third-world countries).

5. What sort of message does this spin on "goodness" give to nonbelievers? What reaction do you think nonbelievers would have upon hearing the truth that God's righteousness can't be earned, but is received only by believing? How does the phrase "you get what you pay for" influence the way nonbelievers perceive what it takes to get into heaven?

More to Consider: Romans 3:23 is a very familiar piece of Scripture that states "all have sinned and fall short of the glory of God." In what ways does this verse directly challenge the popular belief about what it takes to get into heaven?

From the Commentary

Faith is only as good as its object. All people trust something, if only themselves, but the Christian trusts Christ.

—*Be Right*, page 46

6. What sorts of things do people put their faith in (apart from God)? As you consider these, how does Wiersbe's excerpted statement hold true? Why can Christians "boast" of their faith in Christ? What does that really mean?

From the Commentary

Salvation is free, but it is not cheap.

—*Be Right*, page 47

7. Respond to Wiersbe's statement. Now go through Romans 3:21—4:25 and circle anything Paul writes to support this truth. What does it mean that salvation isn't cheap? What is the cost of salvation?

From the Commentary

> God must be perfectly consistent with Himself. He cannot break His own law or violate His own nature. "God is love" (1 John 4:8), and "God is light" (1 John 1:5). A God of love wants to forgive sinners, but a God of holiness must punish sin and uphold His righteous law. How can God be both "just and the justifier"? The answer is in Jesus Christ.
>
> —*Be Right*, pages 48–49

8. Why is it difficult sometimes for Christians to reconcile the "love" and "righteousness" of God? How does Paul defend Jesus Christ as the answer to this difficult question?

From the Commentary

> The fact that Abraham was justified by grace and not law proves that salvation is for all. Abraham is the father of all believers, both Jews and Gentiles (Rom. 4:16; Gal. 3:7, 29). Instead of the Jew complaining because Abraham was not saved by law, he ought to rejoice that God's salvation is available to all men, and that Abraham has a spiritual family (all true believers) as well as a physical family (the

nation of Israel). Paul saw this as a fulfillment of Genesis 17:5: "A father of many nations have I made thee."

—*Be Right*, page 52

9. Why might the Jews complain that Abraham wasn't saved by the law? Would there be a need for a Messiah if he hadn't been saved by the law? Why or why not? Why do you think Jews don't rejoice that Abraham was saved by grace? Why ought we as Christians rejoice in this truth?

From the Commentary

> But Abraham did not walk by sight; he walked by faith. What God promises, He performs. All we need do is believe. Abraham's initial faith in God as recorded in Genesis 15 did not diminish in the years that followed. In Genesis 17—18, Abraham was "strong in faith." It was this faith that gave him strength to beget a son in his old age.
>
> The application to salvation is clear: God must wait until the sinner is "dead" and unable to help himself before He can release His saving power.
>
> —*Be Right*, page 53

10. Respond to Wiersbe's statement that "God must wait until the sinner

is 'dead' … before He can release His saving power." When is man "dead"? How does this play out in Abraham's story? In the story of all humankind?

Looking Inward

Take a moment to reflect on all that you've explored thus far in this study of Romans 3:21—4:25. Review your notes and answers and think about how each of these things matters in your life today.

> *Tips for Small Groups: To get the most out of this section, form pairs or trios and have group members take turns answering these questions. Be honest and as open as you can in this discussion, but most of all, be encouraging and supportive of others. Be sensitive to those who are going through particularly difficult times and don't press for people to speak if they're uncomfortable doing so.*

11. What does it mean to you to know you are "justified by faith"? What does being justified "feel" like? What are the evidences of justification in your life?

12. What are some things you've put your faith in that have let you down? What have they taught you about faith? Do you ever feel let down by God? Why or why not? What is more likely: that God has let you down or that

you somehow are missing out on what God is really doing in your life? Is it easy to put your faith in an invisible God? Why or why not?

13. How might your life be different if you had only the law to pursue in order to become righteous? How does God's grace change the way you live your life?

Going Forward

14. Think of one or two things that you have learned that you'd like to work on in the coming week. Remember that this is all about quality, not quantity. It's better to work on one specific area of life and do it well than to work on many and do poorly (or to be so overwhelmed that you simply don't try).

Do you need to work on accepting the once-and-final-ness of your justification by faith? Do you need to work on putting your faith in Christ alone? Be specific. Go back through Romans 3:21—4:25 and put a star next to the phrase or verse that is most encouraging to you. Consider memorizing this verse.

Real-Life Application Ideas: Read Deuteronomy and make a mental note of all the laws that man had to follow in order to become righteous before God. Then give these laws a modern spin and imagine how your life might be different today had Jesus not yet arrived as the Messiah. Talk with a Jewish friend about how he or she approaches what it means to become righteous before God. Then be sure to pray for your Jewish friends to see Jesus as the Messiah so they, too, might know and receive justification by faith.

Seeking Help

15. Write a prayer below (or simply pray one in silence), inviting God to work on your mind and heart in those areas you've previously noted. Be honest about your desires and fears.

Notes for Small Groups:
- *Look for ways to put into practice the things you wrote in the "Going Forward" section in this lesson. Talk with other group members about your ideas and commit to being accountable to one another.*
- *During the coming week, ask the Holy Spirit to continue to reveal truth to you from what you've read and studied.*
- *Before you start the next lesson, read Romans 5:1–21. For more in-depth lesson preparation, read chapter 4, "Live Like a King!" in* Be Right.

By Faith
(ROMANS 5:1–21)

Before you begin ...
- *Pray for the Holy Spirit to reveal truth and wisdom as you go through this lesson.*
- *Read Romans 5:1–21. This lesson references chapter 4 in* Be Right. *It will be helpful for you to have your Bible and a copy of the commentary available as you work through this lesson.*

Getting Started

From the Commentary

[Paul] has explained that God's way of salvation has always been "by grace, through faith" (Eph. 2:8–9), and he has used Abraham as his illustration. If a reader of the letter stopped at this point, he would know that he needed to and could be saved.

But there is much more the sinner needs to know about justification by faith. Can he be sure that it will last? How

is it possible for God to save a sinner through the death of
Christ on the cross?

—Be Right, page 59

1. Do you resonate with the questions Wiersbe poses in the excerpt about
"justification by faith"? As you read Romans 5:1–21, what other questions
did you have about this important concept?

*More to Consider: How does the phrase "once saved, always saved" line
up (or not) with Paul's contention that justification happens only once?*

2. Choose one verse or phrase from Romans 5:1–21 that stands out to you.
This could be something you're intrigued by, something that makes you
uncomfortable, something that puzzles you, something that resonates with
you, or just something you want to examine further. Write that here. What
strikes you about this verse?

Going Deeper

From the Commentary

> Our justification is not simply a guarantee of heaven, as thrilling as that is, but it is also the source of tremendous blessings that we enjoy here and now.
>
> —*Be Right*, page 60

3. What are some of the blessings we enjoy "here and now" from justification? Underline phrases or words that Paul uses to imply or suggest our earthly blessings. God doesn't promise the same kinds of blessings to each person. How would Christianity look different if there were no "here and now" blessings and only the blessing of heaven?

From the Commentary

> Condemnation means that God declares us sinners, which is a declaration of war. Justification means that God declares us righteous, which is a declaration of peace, made possible by Christ's death on the cross. "Mercy and truth are met together; righteousness and peace have kissed each other" (Ps. 85:10). "Because the law worketh wrath" (Rom. 4:15), nobody condemned by the law can enjoy peace with God. But when you are justified by

faith, you are declared righteous, and the law cannot condemn you or declare war!

—*Be Right*, page 60

4. Respond to Paul's comment that "the law worketh wrath." Why does the law condemn? In what ways do you see the "battle" that is being waged by the condemnation of the law?

From Today's World

The highest ranking officials in our government are almost always surrounded by security, and the chances of a common citizen getting an opportunity to have a casual or serious conversation with them is next to zero. This is, of course, a matter of safety and practicality—no one "king" or leader would have time to sit down with every one of his "subjects," therefore we elect representatives to speak on our behalf. It is a good system for government, but far from perfect for the individual.

5. Imagine what it would look like if every American citizen were invited to the White House to talk with the president—one-on-one. How might that change the way each person feels about his or her contribution to society? About how he or she views the president? How does justification open that door in our relationship with God?

From the Commentary

> Justification is no escape from the trials of life. "In the world ye shall have tribulation" (John 16:33). But for the believer, trials work for him and not against him. No amount of suffering can separate us from the Lord (Rom. 8:35–39); instead, trials bring us closer to the Lord and make us more like the Lord. Suffering builds Christian character.
>
> —*Be Right*, page 61

6. Describe some of the "life trials" you have observed in your life and in the lives of those you know. In what ways is it a comfort to know that no amount of suffering can separate us from God? According to Paul, why do trials bring us closer to God? Is it easy to embrace this truth? Why or why not?

More to Consider: Compare and contrast Adam's sin (and how it impacted many) with Jesus' sacrifice (and how it also impacted many).

From the Commentary

> Faith (Rom. 5:1), hope (Rom. 5:2), and love (Rom. 5:5) all combine to give the believer patience in the trials of

life. And patience makes it possible for the believer to grow in character and become a mature child of God (James 1:1–4).

—*Be Right*, page 62

7. How do faith, hope, and love give patience? What does that sort of patience look like? How does the character growth Wiersbe mentions in this excerpt manifest itself in a believer's life?

From the Commentary

Jesus Christ wrote us into His will, and He wrote the will with His blood. "This cup is the new testament in my blood, which is shed for you" (Luke 22:20). He died so that the will would be in force, but then He arose from the dead and returned to heaven that He might enforce the will Himself and distribute the inheritance. Thus, we are "saved by his life."

—*Be Right*, page 63

8. What does it mean to be "saved by [Jesus'] life"? Does the imagery Wiersbe uses of being written into Jesus' will help you understand this idea? Explain.

From the Commentary

> Skeptics sometimes ask, "Was it fair for God to condemn the whole world just because of one man's disobedience?" The answer, of course, is that it was not only fair, but it was also wise and gracious. To begin with, if God had tested each human being individually, the result would have been the same: disobedience. But even more important, by condemning the human race through one man (Adam), God was then able to save the human race through one Man (Jesus Christ)!
>
> —*Be Right*, page 64

9. What is your immediate response to the skeptic's question as previously noted? Do you agree that all humans would have failed and disobeyed? Why is this significant to the theology Paul is presenting in Romans?

From the Commentary

> Grace was not an addition to God's plan; grace was a part of God's plan from the very beginning. God dealt with Adam and Eve in grace; He dealt with the patriarchs in grace; and He dealt with the nation of Israel in grace. He gave the law through Moses, not to replace His grace, but

to reveal man's need for grace. Law was temporary, but
grace is eternal.

—*Be Right*, page 67

10. How did God deal with Adam and Eve in grace? The patriarchs? The
nation of Israel? In what specific ways does the Law reveal man's need for
grace?

Looking Inward

Take a moment to reflect on all that you've explored thus far in this study
of Romans 5:1–21. Review your notes and answers and think about how
each of these things matters in your life today.

> *Tips for Small Groups: To get the most out of this section, form pairs
> or trios and have group members take turns answering these questions.
> Be honest and as open as you can in this discussion, but most of all, be
> encouraging and supportive of others. Be sensitive to those who are
> going through particularly difficult times and don't press for people to
> speak if they're uncomfortable doing so.*

11. What are some specific examples in your life where you are "condemned
by the law"? How does that make you feel about being justified by faith? Do
you sometimes feel that you have to be "rejustified"? How do Paul's words
provide an answer for that feeling?

12. What are some of the greatest trials you've faced in life? In what ways did they threaten to move you away from God? In what ways did they bring you closer to Him? How have you grown because of these trials?

13. Think about what God's grace looks like in your life. What choices or circumstances make you the most thankful for God's grace? Are there areas of your life where you desperately need God's grace? What would it take to receive that grace?

Going Forward

14. Think of one or two things that you have learned that you'd like to work on in the coming week. Remember that this is all about quality, not quantity. It's better to work on one specific area of life and do it well than to work on many and do poorly (or to be so overwhelmed that you simply don't try).

Do you need to better understand what it means to be justified by faith? Do you need to learn to accept God's grace in difficult circumstances? Be specific. Go back through Romans 5:1–21 and put a star next to the phrase or verse that is most encouraging to you. Consider memorizing this verse.

Real-Life Application Ideas: Take a random survey of friends and neighbors (believers and nonbelievers alike), asking them what they think it takes to get into heaven. Then ask them what's most important about our lives here on earth. Compare these responses with what Paul says in Romans 5. Spend a little time in prayer, asking God to prepare you for those opportunities that may come to help people see the truth of God's gift of grace.

Seeking Help

15. Write a prayer below (or simply pray one in silence), inviting God to work on your mind and heart in those areas you've previously noted. Be honest about your desires and fears.

Notes for Small Groups:
- *Look for ways to put into practice the things you wrote in the "Going Forward" section in this lesson. Talk with other group members about your ideas and commit to being accountable to one another.*
- *During the coming week, ask the Holy Spirit to continue to reveal truth to you from what you've read and studied.*
- *Before you start the next lesson, read Romans 6:1–23. For more in-depth lesson preparation, read chapter 5, "Dying to Live," in* Be Right.

Responding to Objections

(ROMANS 6:1–23)

Before you begin …

- *Pray for the Holy Spirit to reveal truth and wisdom as you go through this lesson.*
- *Read Romans 6:1–23. This lesson references chapter 5 in* Be Right. *It will be helpful for you to have your Bible and a copy of the commentary available as you work through this lesson.*

Getting Started

From the Commentary

In Romans 6—8 Paul defended his doctrine of justification by faith. He anticipated three objections: (1) "If God's grace abounds when we sin, then let's continue sinning so we might experience more grace" (Rom. 6:1–14); (2) "If we are no longer under the law, then we are free to live as we please" (Rom. 6:15—7:6); and (3) "You have made God's law sinful" (Rom. 7:7–25).

—Be Right, *page 71*

1. What are your thoughts about the objections listed in the excerpt? Do you agree these are worthy questions to ask about Paul's teaching? Why would these have been of particular importance to the audience Paul was addressing (the church in Rome)?

More to Consider: In Romans 3:21—5:21, Paul refers to "sins" and then in chapters 6—8, he starts talking about the principle of "sin." What is significant about this shift?

2. Choose one verse or phrase from Romans 6:1–23 that stands out to you. This could be something you're intrigued by, something that makes you uncomfortable, something that puzzles you, something that resonates with you, or just something you want to examine further. Write that here. What strikes you about this verse?

Going Deeper

From the Commentary

The repetition of the word *know* in Romans 6:3, 6, and 9 indicates that Paul wanted us to understand a basic doctrine. Christian living depends on Christian learning; duty is always founded on doctrine. If Satan can keep a Christian ignorant, he can keep him impotent.

—*Be Right*, pages 71–72

3. Why does Christian living depend on learning? What sort of learning do you think Paul is referring to? Do you agree that an ignorant Christian is an impotent Christian? Explain.

From the Commentary

Historians agree that the mode of baptism in the early church was immersion. The believer was "buried" in the water and brought up again as a picture of death, burial, and resurrection. Baptism by immersion (which is the illustration Paul is using in Rom. 6) pictures the believer's identification with Christ in His death, burial, and resurrection. It is an outward symbol of an inward experience. Paul is not saying that their immersion in water put them "into Jesus Christ," for that was accomplished by the Spirit when they believed. Their immersion was a picture of what the Spirit did: the Holy Spirit identified them with Christ in His death, burial, and resurrection.

—*Be Right*, page 73

4. What is your church's perspective on baptism? In what ways does it line up with what Paul writes? If baptism is merely a symbol, is it necessary for Christians? Why or why not? What happens at baptism?

From Today's World

Plenty of products today are being sold that promise to "change your life." This includes everything from shampoo to a new car. Advertisements for these products can often seem unbelievable because of the spoken or implied claims. But in reality, there are few things that can truly, radically change a person's life.

5. When you think about the symbol of baptism and what it represents, how does this compare to the promises presented by the advertising world? Why can we, as Christians, count on the life-changing nature of justification by faith? How then should we live if we have been changed?

From the Commentary

> Too many Christians are "betweeners": they live between Egypt and Canaan, saved but never satisfied; or they live between Good Friday and Easter, believing in the cross but not entering into the power and glory of the resurrection.

Romans 6:5 indicates that our union with Christ assures our future resurrection should we die. But Romans 6:4 teaches that we share His resurrection power today.

—*Be Right*, page 74

6. What does it look like to be a "betweener" in today's church culture? Why is "being saved" enough for some people? What are ways Christians can share in Jesus' resurrection power today?

More to Consider: What is Paul's response to believers who claim that his theology leaves opportunity for believers to sin willingly since they have already been given their new lives?

From the Commentary

Sin is a terrible master, and it finds a willing servant in the human body. The body is not sinful; the body is neutral. It can be controlled either by sin or by God. But man's fallen nature, which is not changed at conversion, gives sin a beachhead from which it can attack and then control. Paul expressed the problem: "For I know that in me (that is, in my flesh) dwelleth no good thing: for to will is present with me; but how to perform that which is good I find not" (Rom. 7:18).

—*Be Right*, page 75

7. What are your thoughts about Wiersbe's comment that "the body is neutral"? What are the "beachheads" that sin uses to attack us? How can we shore up defenses against sin's encroaching ways?

From the Commentary

There must be in the believer's life that final and complete surrender of the body to Jesus Christ. This does not mean there will be no further steps of surrender, because there will be. The longer we walk with Christ, the deeper the fellowship must become. But there can be no subsequent steps without that first step.

—*Be Right*, page 77

8. What is that "final and complete surrender of the body" Wiersbe describes in this excerpt? What does Paul say about this? If there is a "final surrender," how can there then be further steps of surrender?

More to Consider: Circle every time Paul uses the word yield *in Romans 6:12–23 (KJV). Why do you think he uses this word so frequently?*

From the Commentary

> Before you were saved, you were the slave of sin. Now that you belong to Christ, you are freed from that old slavery and made the servant of Christ. Romans 6:19 suggests that the Christian ought to be as enthusiastic in yielding to the Lord as he was in yielding to sin. A friend once said to me, "I want to be as good a saint as I was a sinner!"
>
> —*Be Right*, pages 78–79

9. Is it easy to be enthusiastic about yielding? Why or why not? What does it take to be "as good a saint as you were a sinner"?

From the Commentary

> In the old life, we produced fruit that made us ashamed. In the new life in Christ, we produce fruit that glorifies God and brings joy to our lives.
>
> —*Be Right*, page 79

10. What are some examples of fruit that makes us ashamed? Compare that to the fruit that glorifies God and brings joy. What is different about these types of fruit?

Looking Inward

Take a moment to reflect on all that you've explored thus far in this study of Romans 6:1–23. Review your notes and answers and think about how each of these things matters in your life today.

> *Tips for Small Groups: To get the most out of this section, form pairs or trios and have group members take turns answering these questions. Be honest and as open as you can in this discussion, but most of all, be encouraging and supportive of others. Be sensitive to those who are going through particularly difficult times and don't press for people to speak if they're uncomfortable doing so.*

11. What are some ways you're learning so you can live a better Christian life? Are there some things you're not doing that you could be doing? List these, then make a plan to work on them in the coming week.

12. Have you been baptized? If no, why not? If yes, what does that baptism mean to you? If you were saved when you were justified by faith, why is your baptism still important?

13. How are you currently living a life yielded to God? What are some areas of your life where you aren't yielded to God? Why are these difficult areas for you? What would it take to yield them to God?

Going Forward

14. Think of one or two things that you have learned that you'd like to work on in the coming week. Remember that this is all about quality, not quantity. It's better to work on one specific area of life and do it well than to work on many and do poorly (or to be so overwhelmed that you simply don't try).

Do you need to spend more time studying so you won't be an impotent Christian? Do you need to work on yielding to God? Be specific. Go back through Romans 6:1–23 and put a star next to the phrase or verse that is most encouraging to you. Consider memorizing this verse.

Real-Life Application Ideas: If you haven't been baptized, talk with your pastor about what you need to do to consider baptism in your church. If you have been baptized, revisit that experience and take a few moments to reflect on the symbolism of that action and what it means to you. Then write out a prayer of thanksgiving to God for the symbol and how it can help you know what it means to live a new life in Christ.

Seeking Help

15. Write a prayer below (or simply pray one in silence), inviting God to work on your mind and heart in those areas you've previously noted. Be honest about your desires and fears.

Notes for Small Groups:
- *Look for ways to put into practice the things you wrote in the "Going Forward" section in this lesson. Talk with other group members about your ideas and commit to being accountable to one another.*
- *During the coming week, ask the Holy Spirit to continue to reveal truth to you from what you've read and studied.*
- *Before you start the next lesson, read Romans 7:1–25. For more in-depth lesson preparation, read chapter 6, "Christians and the Law," in* Be Right.

The Law
(ROMANS 7:1–25)

Before you begin …
- *Pray for the Holy Spirit to reveal truth and wisdom as you go through this lesson.*
- *Read Romans 7:1–25. This lesson references chapter 6 in* Be Right. *It will be helpful for you to have your Bible and a copy of the commentary available as you work through this lesson.*

Getting Started

From the Commentary

What really is legalism? It is the belief that I can become holy and please God by obeying laws. It is measuring spirituality by a list of dos and don'ts. The weakness of legalism is that it sees *sins* (plural) but not *sin* (the root of the trouble). It judges by the outward and not the inward. Furthermore, the legalist fails to understand the

real purpose of God's law and the relationship between
law and grace.

—*Be Right,* page 84

1. What are your thoughts about Wiersbe's explanation of "the weakness
of legalism"? How does legalism judge by outward actions? What are the
inward truths that legalism misses?

*More to Consider: Paul uses the illustration of a marriage in Romans
7 to show that believers have a new relationship to the law because of
their relationship with Jesus. What is this illustration and why do you
think Paul used marriage to teach this concept?*

2. Choose one verse or phrase from Romans 7:1–25 that stands out to you.
This could be something you're intrigued by, something that makes you
uncomfortable, something that puzzles you, something that resonates with
you, or just something you want to examine further. Write that here.

Going Deeper

From the Commentary

> It appears that Paul has confused his illustration, but he
> has not. When we were unsaved ("in the flesh," Rom. 7:5),
> we were under the authority of God's law. We were con-
> demned by that law. When we trusted Christ and were
> united to Him, *we died to the law* just as we died to the
> flesh (Rom. 6:1–10). The law did not die; *we* died.
>
> —*Be Right*, page 85

3. What is your reaction to the statement that "the Law did not die; we
died"? What does it look like practically speaking when we are no longer
under the authority of the Law? What does it mean to be "united to Christ"?

From the Commentary

> This is the logical conclusion: the law cannot exercise
> authority over a dead person. The Authorized Version
> reads as though the law died, but Paul wrote, "We having
> died to that wherein we were held." Death means deliver-
> ance (note Rom. 6:9–10). But we were delivered that we
> might serve. The Christian life is not one of independence
> and rebellion. We died to the law that we might be "mar-
> ried to Christ." We were delivered from the law that we

might serve Christ. This truth refutes the false accusation
that Paul taught lawlessness.

—*Be Right*, page 86

4. In what ways does the death of our old selves under the law (in favor of life in our new relationship with Christ) equal deliverance? What does Paul say that refutes the idea that he was teaching lawlessness?

From Today's World

Our country still has plenty of old laws on the books that are unenforceable or may just seem silly. For example, in Massachusetts, no gorilla is allowed in the backseat of a car. In Tennessee, it is illegal to drive while sleeping. While these may make us laugh today, at one time the law had a purpose (perhaps prompted by a single, specific incident). The Old Testament gives us a long list of laws that are to be upheld in order to be godly and earn righteousness.

5. What is the purpose of specific laws in our world today? What is the intent of "the law"? In Paul's day, as now, Christians struggle to understand how they are to respond to the laws ordained in the Old Testament. How does Paul explain what our relationship to the law ought to be once we are living under grace?

From the Commentary

> The law is a mirror that reveals the inner man and shows
> us how dirty we are (James 1:22–25). Note that Paul did
> not use murder, stealing, or adultery in his discussion; he
> uses *coveting*.
>
> —*Be Right*, page 87

6. How is the law a mirror? Why do you think Paul focused on "coveting"
while describing this aspect of the law? What is unique about the act of
coveting when compared to the other of the Ten Commandments?

*More to Consider: Wiersbe writes, "Believers who try to live by rules
and regulations discover that their legalistic system only arouses more sin
and creates more problems." Skim Paul's letter to the Galatians (espe-
cially 5:15). How does this letter support what Wiersbe is stating? What
are some of the problems that the Galatian church encountered because
of legalism?*

From the Commentary

> Something in human nature wants to rebel whenever a law is given.
>
> —*Be Right*, page 87

7. Respond to Wiersbe's statement. What are some examples of this in today's culture? (A simple example would be touching something that is clearly marked "fresh paint, don't touch.") Why do you think this is part of our human nature?

From the Commentary

> As the new Christian grows, he comes into contact with various philosophies of the Christian life. He can read books, attend seminars, listen to tapes, and get a great deal of information. If he is not careful, he will start following a human leader and accept his teachings as law. This practice is a very subtle form of legalism, and it kills spiritual growth.
>
> —*Be Right*, page 88

8. Think of some examples of the subtle form of legalism Wiersbe describes in the excerpt, then reread Romans 7:10–11. How can even a good desire

to pursue the truth kill spiritual growth? What is the key to avoiding this kind of legalism?

More to Consider: Think back on the stories of great leaders who led their people astray. Even though their ideas may have started out good (and even biblical), somehow the emphasis shifted and became more about the leader than the greater truth. What are the signs to watch out for that indicate someone is not teaching God's truth, but his or her own brand?

From the Commentary

Our nature is carnal (fleshly), but the law's nature is spiritual. This explains why the old nature responds as it does to the law. It has well been said, "The old nature knows no law, the new nature needs no law." The law cannot transform the old nature; it can only reveal how sinful that old nature is. The believer who tries to live under law will only *activate* the old nature; he will not eradicate it.

—*Be Right*, page 90

9. Think of an example or two of how the law reveals our sinful nature. Why does "the old nature" know no law? Isn't the old nature the one that

tries to earn righteousness through the law? Why does the new nature need no law?

From the Commentary

> The legalist says, "Obey the law and you will do good and live a good life." But the law only reveals and arouses sin, showing how sinful it is! It is impossible for me to obey the law because I have a sinful nature that rebels against the law. Even if I think I have done good, I know that evil is present. The law is good, but by nature, I am bad! So the legalist is wrong: The law cannot enable us to do good.
>
> —*Be Right*, page 91

10. What are some examples of legalism in the world around you (work, church, home)? How is that similar to or different from the legalism Christians must fight against in their Christian walk? Do you agree that the law cannot enable us to do good? Why or why not?

Looking Inward

Take a moment to reflect on all that you've explored thus far in this study of Romans 7:1–25. Review your notes and answers and think about how each of these things matters in your life today.

Tips for Small Groups: To get the most out of this section, form pairs or trios and have group members take turns answering these questions. Be honest and as open as you can in this discussion, but most of all, be encouraging and supportive of others. Be sensitive to those who are going through particularly difficult times and don't press for people to speak if they're uncomfortable doing so.

11. In what ways are you legalistic in your faith-life? What prompts that sort of legalism? What steps do you need to take to avoid legalism and embrace the truth of God's gift of grace?

12. What would the "mirror" of the law reflect about your life today? What are some of the things you're struggling with that illustrate the truth of Paul's teaching about the law?

13. Are you ever tempted to live "lawlessly" because of the surety of your justification by faith? Why or why not? How do Paul's words about the relationship between a believer and the law intersect with the way you're living your life today?

Going Forward

14. Think of one or two things that you have learned that you'd like to work on in the coming week. Remember that this is all about quality, not quantity. It's better to work on one specific area of life and do it well than to work on many and do poorly (or to be so overwhelmed that you simply don't try).

Do you need to become less legalistic? Do you need to learn how to live under the "new nature" you've been given in Christ? Be specific. Go back through Romans 7:1–25 and put a star next to the phrase or verse that is most encouraging to you. Consider memorizing this verse.

Real-Life Application Ideas: Talk with a close friend or family member about how he or she sees you living your life of faith. Invite that person to speak openly and honestly to you about those areas where you might tend toward legalism. Then take time together to think of ways to overcome that tendency and, instead, work on the inward attitudes that reflect a life dedicated to Christ.

Seeking Help

15. Write a prayer below (or simply pray one in silence), inviting God to work on your mind and heart in those areas you've previously noted. Be honest about your desires and fears.

Notes for Small Groups:

- *Look for ways to put into practice the things you wrote in the "Going Forward" section in this lesson. Talk with other group members about your ideas and commit to being accountable to one another.*
- *During the coming week, ask the Holy Spirit to continue to reveal truth to you from what you've read and studied.*
- *Before you start the next lesson, read Romans 8:1–39. For more in-depth lesson preparation, read chapter 7, "Freedom and Fulfillment," in* Be Right.

Spirit and Freedom

(ROMANS 8:1–39)

Before you begin …

- *Pray for the Holy Spirit to reveal truth and wisdom as you go through this lesson.*
- *Read Romans 8:1–39. This lesson references chapter 7 in* Be Right. *It will be helpful for you to have your Bible and a copy of the commentary available as you work through this lesson.*

Getting Started

From the Commentary

Romans 8 is the Christian's "Declaration of Freedom," for in it Paul declares the four spiritual freedoms we enjoy because of our union with Jesus Christ. A study of this chapter shows the emphasis on the Holy Spirit, who is mentioned nineteen times. "Where the Spirit of the Lord is, there is liberty" (2 Cor. 3:17).

—*Be Right,* page 97

1. What are the four spiritual freedoms Paul talks about in Romans 8? What is your reaction to the gift of this freedom, offered to those who follow Jesus?

More to Consider: Wiersbe writes, "The 'law of double jeopardy' states that a man cannot be tried twice for the same crime." How is this law like the truth afforded us by Jesus' payment for our sins on the cross?

2. Choose one verse or phrase from Romans 8:1–39 that stands out to you. This could be something you're intrigued by, something that makes you uncomfortable, something that puzzles you, something that resonates with you, or just something you want to examine further. Write that here. What strikes you about this verse?

Going Deeper

3. Go through Romans 8 and circle all of Paul's references to the Spirit. What does this tell you about the role of the Spirit for those who are no longer under the law? What are some of the things the Spirit does on our behalf?

From the Commentary

> The legalist tries to obey God in his own strength and fails to measure up to the righteousness that God demands. The Spirit-led Christian, as he yields to the Lord, experiences the sanctifying work of the Spirit in his life.
>
> —*Be Right*, page 99

4. How do Christians go about "yielding" to the Lord? What is the sanctifying work of the Spirit?

From Today's World

The world does not recognize that there is a difference between things "of the flesh" and things "of the Spirit." In fact, most of what is presented to Americans today through the media and advertising promises to satisfy only fleshly desires. Take a moment to recall the various messages that have passed before you today (in magazines, on the radio, television, or Internet, in advertising). Consider the point and purpose of those messages.

5. What was the purpose of those messages you've recalled? In what ways do they speak to fleshly desires? Does this mean that all popular media is bad? Why or why not? What changes when you view these images or hear these messages through the filter of faith (a life fixed on the things of the Spirit)? How do you go about doing that?

From the Commentary

> To be "in the flesh" means to be lost, outside Christ. The
> unsaved person lives to please himself and rarely if ever
> thinks about pleasing God. The root of sin is selfishness—
> "I will" and not "Thy will."
>
> —*Be Right*, page 100

6. What are some ways unsaved people live to please themselves? What are
the greatest temptations Christians face to do the same thing? How does one
turn from desiring to please only him- or herself to desiring to please God?

*More to Consider: Read 1 Corinthians 6:19–20. How does this pas-
sage speak to the way in which we are to live as men and women who
have the Holy Spirit within us?*

From the Commentary

> What a difference it makes in your body when the Holy
> Spirit lives within. You experience new life, and even your
> physical faculties take on a new dimension of experience.
> When evangelist D. L. Moody described his conversion
> experience, he said: "I was in a new world. The next

morning the sun shone brighter and the birds sang sweeter ... the old elms waved their branches for joy, and all nature was at peace." Life in Christ is abundant life.

—*Be Right*, pages 100–101

7. What does the "new world" of a life with the Holy Spirit look like? In what ways do you see this life as abundant? How is this lived out and in evidence in your church or other community of believers? Why is it important to recognize this "new dimension" offered by the Spirit? How can our recognition and embracing of the Spirit's role in our lives impact the lives of those around us?

From the Commentary

Today the Holy Spirit groans with us and feels the burdens of our weaknesses and suffering. But the Spirit does more than groan. He prays for us in His groaning so that we might be led into the will of God. We do not always know God's will. We do not always know how to pray, but the Spirit intercedes so that we might live in the will of God in spite of suffering. The Spirit "shares the burden."

—*Be Right*, page 103

8. Why is it important to know that the Holy Spirit "groans" with us? What are the other roles of the Holy Spirit as expressed by Paul in Romans 8?

More to Consider: Respond to this Wiersbe quote: "We do not need to fear the past, present, or future because we are secure in the love of Christ."

From the Commentary

The believer needs to enter into each new day realizing that God is for him. There is no need to fear, for his loving Father desires only the best for His children, even if they must go through trials to receive His best.

—*Be Right*, page 105

9. How does the belief that "God is for us" help us when we're facing difficult circumstances or trials? Is it always easy to believe God is for you? Why or why not? What sort of spiritual growth comes from trusting God that has our best interests in mind?

From the Commentary

> God does not shelter us from the difficulties of life because we need them for our spiritual growth (Rom. 5:3–5). In Romans 8:28 God assures us that the difficulties of life are working *for* us and not *against* us. God permits trials to come that we might use them for our good and His glory. We endure trials for His sake (Rom. 8:36), and since we do, do you think that He will desert us? Of course not! Instead, He is closer to us when we go through the difficulties of life.
>
> —*Be Right*, page 106

10. What does it look like to endure trials for God's sake? How is God closer during these times? Does God *feel* closer during these times? Why or why not?

Looking Inward

Take a moment to reflect on all that you've explored thus far in this study of Romans 8:1–39. Review your notes and answers and think about how each of these things matters in your life today.

Tips for Small Groups: To get the most out of this section, form pairs or trios and have group members take turns answering these questions.

Be honest and as open as you can in this discussion, but most of all, be encouraging and supportive of others. Be sensitive to those who are going through particularly difficult times and don't press for people to speak if they're uncomfortable doing so.

11. What does it mean to you to know that the Holy Spirit is "groaning" on your behalf? What are some of the life circumstances you're facing that cause you to look to the Holy Spirit for guidance and help? How are Paul's words in this chapter of Romans encouraging to you?

12. What are some ways you still try to "please self" instead of "please God"? What drives those desires? What would it take to trust the Holy Spirit to help you with those areas that are still driven by pleasing yourself?

13. Is it easy for you to believe God is "for" you? Why or why not? When is it most challenging for you to trust that God's purposes are for your good? According to Paul, what is the Holy Spirit's role in helping you to believe and embrace this truth?

Going Forward

14. Think of one or two things that you have learned that you'd like to work on in the coming week. Remember that this is all about quality, not quantity. It's better to work on one specific area of life and do it well than to work on many and do poorly (or to be so overwhelmed that you simply don't try).

Do you need to learn more about the role of the Holy Spirit in your life? Embrace the freedom offered by the Spirit? Turn from pleasing self to pleasing God? Be specific. Go back through Romans 8:1–39 and put a star next to the phrase or verse that is most encouraging to you. Consider memorizing this verse.

Real-Life Application Ideas: The Holy Spirit plays a variety of roles in a believer's life. Take some time this week to learn more about the Holy Spirit. You can do this in a variety of ways: simply by studying the Bible (use a concordance to search for "Spirit" or a Bible dictionary to track down key verses); reading books on the Holy Spirit; or talking with a pastor or other church leader.

Seeking Help

15. Write a prayer below (or simply pray one in silence), inviting God to work on your mind and heart in those areas you've previously noted. Be honest about your desires and fears.

Notes for Small Groups:

- *Look for ways to put into practice the things you wrote in the "Going Forward" section in this lesson. Talk with other group members about your ideas and commit to being accountable to one another.*

- *During the coming week, ask the Holy Spirit to continue to reveal truth to you from what you've read and studied.*

- *Before you start the next lesson, read Romans 9:1–33. For more in-depth lesson preparation, read chapter 8, "Did God Make a Mistake?" in* Be Right.

Israel's Past
(ROMANS 9:1–33)

Before you begin …
- *Pray for the Holy Spirit to reveal truth and wisdom as you go through this lesson.*
- *Read Romans 9:1–33. This lesson references chapter 8 in* Be Right. *It will be helpful for you to have your Bible and a copy of the commentary available as you work through this lesson.*

Getting Started

From the Commentary

Paul argued in Romans 8 that the believer is secure in Jesus Christ and that God's election would stand (Rom. 8:28–30). But someone might ask, "What about the Jews? They were chosen by God, and yet now you tell us they are set aside and God is building His church. Did God fail to keep His promises to Israel?" In other words, the very character of God was at stake. If God was not faithful to the Jews, how do we know He will be faithful to the church?

—*Be Right,* pages 111–12

1. Why do you think Paul took this break from doctrinal teaching to talk about the original role of the Israelites in God's plan? How does this chapter fit with the larger theme of Romans?

More to Consider: Read about God's election of Israel as His people in Exodus 4:22–23, 40:34–38, and 1 Kings 8:10–11. How does this play into Paul's teaching in Romans 9?

2. Choose one verse or phrase from Romans 9:1–33 that stands out to you. This could be something you're intrigued by, something that makes you uncomfortable, something that puzzles you, something that resonates with you, or just something you want to examine further. Write that here. What strikes you about this verse?

Going Deeper

From the Commentary

> It is remarkable how Paul moved from the joy of Romans
> 8 into the sorrow and burden of Romans 9. When he
> looked at Christ, he rejoiced, but when he looked at the
> lost people of Israel, he wept. Like Moses (Ex. 32:30–35),
> he was willing to be cursed and separated from Christ if it
> would mean the salvation of Israel. What a man this Paul
> was! He was willing to stay out of heaven for the sake of
> the saved (Phil. 1:22–24), and willing to go to hell for the
> sake of the lost.
>
> —*Be Right*, page 112

3. What is your reaction to Paul's sorrow over Israel? How do you feel about
Paul's words in Romans 9:3? What drives Paul's passion about the nation of
Israel?

From the Commentary

> "Is there unrighteousness with God?" Paul asked, and then
> he replied, "God forbid!" It is unthinkable that the holy
> God should ever commit an unrighteous act. Election is

always totally a matter of grace. If God acted only on the
basis of righteousness, nobody would ever be saved.

—*Be Right*, page 114

4. What does Wiersbe mean by the word *election*? Respond to his statement
about election being totally a matter of grace. Why would no one be saved
if God acted only on the basis of righteousness? Why is this truth critical
to what Paul teaches in Romans 9?

From Today's World

In a world driven by political correctness, the idea that "everyone is entitled
to his or her religious beliefs" is sometimes interpreted as "everyone is right."
This sort of thinking might support the idea of tolerance, but it goes against
the very nature of a Holy God who must punish sin in order for Him to be
holy and yet desires for people to be saved from sin.

5. How does a believer's faith intersect with the world's view on religious
beliefs? Does "political correctness" mesh well with what you know about
God as written in Romans? Why or why not? How can Christians be "in
the world but not of it" when it comes to living out the truth of (and telling
others about) God's "sovereign election"?

From the Commentary

God is holy and must punish sin, but God is loving and desires to save sinners. If everybody is saved, it would deny His holiness, but if everybody is lost, it would deny His love. The solution to the problem is God's sovereign election.

A seminary professor once said to me, "Try to explain election, and you may lose your mind; but explain it away and you will lose your soul!"

—*Be Right*, pages 114–15

6. Circle the words Paul uses in this chapter that tell about God's original plan for the Israelites. Then underline those words that illustrate God's grace. How do God's mercy and justice work together in this?

From the Commentary

God is wiser than we are, and we are foolish to question His will or to resist it. (The reference here is to Isa. 45:9.) To be sure, the clay has no life and is passive in the potter's hand. We have feelings, intellect, and willpower, and we can resist Him if we choose. (See Jer. 18, where this thought is developed.) But it is God who determines whether a man will be a Moses or a Pharaoh.

—*Be Right*, page 116

7. What is the importance of man's ability to resist God in Paul's teaching about the Israelites? Why do men still choose to resist or question God's will? What was the Israelites' reason for resisting God?

From the Commentary

God prepares men for glory (Rom. 9:23), but sinners prepare themselves for judgment. In Moses and Israel, God revealed the riches of His mercy; in Pharaoh and Egypt, He revealed His power and wrath. Since neither deserved any mercy, God cannot be charged with injustice.

—*Be Right*, page 117

8. In what ways does God prepare men for glory? How do sinners prepare themselves for judgment? How was this true in Paul's day? Today?

More to Consider: Wiersbe writes that "at the exodus, God rejected the Gentiles and chose the Jews, so that, through the Jews, He might save the Gentiles." According to Paul, how did God save the Gentiles through the Jews?

From the Commentary

> Paul moved next from divine sovereignty to human responsibility. Note that Paul did not say "elect" and "nonelect," but rather emphasized faith. Here is a paradox: the Jews sought righteousness but did not find it, while the Gentiles, who were not searching for it, found it! The reason? Israel tried to be saved by works and not by faith.
>
> —*Be Right*, page 118

9. Why do you think Paul emphasizes "faith" in his discussion of human responsibility instead of "elect" and "nonelect"? What is your response to the paradox Wiersbe describes in the excerpt? How do Christians today sometimes attempt to be saved by works and not by faith? What does a "responsible faith" look like?

From the Commentary

No one will deny that there are many mysteries connected

with divine sovereignty and human responsibility. Nowhere does God ask us to choose between these two truths, because they both come from God and are a part of God's plan. They do not compete; they cooperate. The fact that we cannot fully understand *how* they work together does not deny the fact that they do. When a man asked Charles Spurgeon how he reconciled divine sovereignty and human responsibility, Spurgeon replied, "I never try to reconcile friends!"

—*Be Right*, page 119

10. What is the greatest challenge in understanding the paradox of sovereignty and responsibility? How do they "cooperate"?

Looking Inward

Take a moment to reflect on all that you've explored thus far in this study of Romans 9:1–33. Review your notes and answers and think about how each of these things matters in your life today.

Tips for Small Groups: To get the most out of this section, form pairs or trios and have group members take turns answering these questions. Be honest and as open as you can in this discussion, but most of all, be encouraging and supportive of others. Be sensitive to those who are going through particularly difficult times and don't press for people to speak if they're uncomfortable doing so.

11. Paul quotes God's words to Moses in this chapter, reminding readers that God has mercy and compassion on those whom He chooses. What is your emotional reaction to this? How do you factor this in with your own faith story?

12. How do you feel about the truth that because of God's holiness, not everyone will get into heaven? Who are the people in your life who don't yet know Christ? What are some things you can do now to help them see what a life of faith might be like? What are some other things you can do to help people you care about come to Christ?

13. What does God's mercy look like in your life? How do you show your thankfulness to God for electing you? What does it mean to you to be responsible with the faith you've been given? How does that play out in everyday life?

Going Forward

14. Think of one or two things that you have learned that you'd like to work on in the coming week. Remember that this is all about quality, not quantity. It's better to work on one specific area of life and do it well than to work on many and do poorly (or to be so overwhelmed that you simply don't try).

Do you need to learn more about God's holiness? Embrace the responsibilities that come with being "elected" by God? Be specific. Go back through Romans 9:1–33 and put a star next to the phrase or verse that is most encouraging to you. Consider memorizing this verse.

Real-Life Application Ideas: Interview one or more Jewish friends about their understanding of this chapter in Romans. Then spend some time in the coming weeks praying specifically for your Jewish friends— that they might see the truth of Christ's role as Messiah and choose to follow Him.

Seeking Help

15. Write a prayer below (or simply pray one in silence), inviting God to work on your mind and heart in those areas you've previously noted. Be honest about your desires and fears.

Notes for Small Groups:

- *Look for ways to put into practice the things you wrote in the "Going Forward" section in this lesson. Talk with other group members about your ideas and commit to being accountable to one another.*

- *During the coming week, ask the Holy Spirit to continue to reveal truth to you from what you've read and studied.*

- *Before you start the next lesson, read Romans 10:1–21. For more in-depth lesson preparation, read chapter 9, "The Wrong Righteousness," in* Be Right.

Rejection
(ROMANS 10:1–21)

Before you begin ...
- *Pray for the Holy Spirit to reveal truth and wisdom as you go through this lesson.*
- *Read Romans 10:1–21. This lesson references chapter 9 in* Be Right. *It will be helpful for you to have your Bible and a copy of the commentary available as you work through this lesson.*

Getting Started

From the Commentary

You would think that Israel as a nation would have been eagerly expecting the arrival of their Messiah and been prepared to receive Him. For centuries they had known the Old Testament prophecies and had practiced the law, which was "a schoolmaster" to lead them to Christ (Gal. 3:24). God had sought to prepare the nation, but when Jesus Christ came, they rejected Him.

—*Be Right,* page 123

1. Why do you think the Israelites rejected Jesus when they were so eager for their Messiah? How is the law a "schoolmaster" or "teacher" to lead the Jews to Christ?

More to Consider: The Jews rejected Jesus in part because many thought they didn't really need a savior (at least not spiritually). They did, however, see the need for political salvation from Rome. How do these truths play into the Israelites' response to Jesus?

2. Choose one verse or phrase from Romans 10:1–21 that stands out to you. This could be something you're intrigued by, something that makes you uncomfortable, something that puzzles you, something that resonates with you, or just something you want to examine further. Write that here. What strikes you about this verse?

Going Deeper

From the Commentary

Ever since Israel returned to their land from Babylonian captivity, the nation had been cured of idolatry. In the temple and the local synagogues, only the true God was worshipped and served, and only the true law was taught. So zealous were the Jews that they even "improved upon God's law" and added their own traditions, making them equal to the law. Paul himself had been zealous for the law and the traditions (Acts 26:1–11; Gal. 1:13–14).

But their zeal was not based on knowledge; it was heat without light.

—*Be Right*, page 124

3. In what ways was the Israelites' zeal "heat without light"? What was the missing "light"? What are some examples of this same sort of thinking even in the church today? What prompts this sort of approach to God?

From the Commentary

There is an ignorance that comes from lack of opportunity, but Israel had had many opportunities to be saved. In their case, it was an ignorance that stemmed from willful, stubborn resistance to the truth. They would not submit to God. They were proud of their own good works and religious self-righteousness and would not admit their sins and trust the Savior.

—*Be Right*, page 124

4. What are some of the opportunities the Israelites had to be saved? Why didn't they take advantage of those opportunities? What are some similar examples of missed opportunities in today's world? How does pride impact the ability of men and women to choose to follow Jesus today?

From Today's World

A few years ago, when the national media reported about a woman who spilled coffee on herself at a fast-food restaurant and then sued that restaurant because the coffee was too hot, the floodgates for questionable or spurious lawsuits was opened wide. Now there are lawsuits filed for just about anything you could imagine, and the litigious people filing these suits hold tight to the belief that they're well within the law to do so.

5. Why would a lawyer take on a questionable or spurious lawsuit? How is this an example of taking advantage of the law for personal gain? In what ways did the Israelites "use" the law for their own benefit? What is the difference between following the "letter of the law" versus following the "spirit of the law"? If the Israelites followed the spirit of the law, how might this have impacted their acceptance or rejection of Jesus as the Messiah?

From the Commentary

> Christ is "the end of the law" in the sense that through
> His death and resurrection, He has terminated the min-
> istry of the law for those who believe. The law is ended as
> far as Christians are concerned. The righteousness of the
> law is being fulfilled in the life of the believer through the
> power of the Spirit (Rom. 8:4), but the reign of the law has
> ended (see Eph. 2:15; Col. 2:14).
>
> —*Be Right*, page 125

6. How is the righteousness of the law fulfilled in believers? What does that
look like? If the reign of the law has ended, how then are Christians sup-
posed to relate to the law?

*More to Consider: Read Ephesians 2:15 and Colossians 2:14. What do
these verses say about the "reign of the law"?*

From the Commentary

> [Paul] told us that God's way of salvation was not difficult
> and complicated. We do not have to go to heaven to find
> Christ, or into the world of the dead. He is near to us. In
> other words, the gospel of Christ—the Word of faith—is

available and accessible. The sinner need not perform difficult works in order to be saved. All he has to do is trust Christ.

—*Be Right*, pages 126

7. In the simplest of terms, what is the "gospel of Christ"? How does someone go about trusting Christ? Why is this difficult for many people?

From the Commentary

Note that trusting Christ is not only a matter of believing, but also obeying. Not to believe in Christ is to disobey God. God "commandeth all men everywhere to repent" (Acts 17:30). Romans 6:17 also equates "believing" and "obeying." True faith must touch the will and result in a changed life.

—*Be Right*, page 128

8. Respond to the following: "True faith must touch the will and result in a changed life." According to Paul, what does this "true faith" look like? What are evidences of the changed life?

More to Consider: The quotation in Romans 10:15 is found in Isaiah 52:7 and Nahum 1:15. Read these references in context. How do they compare to the Romans reference? What does the phrase "beautiful feet" refer to in each of these passages?

From the Commentary

> When Israel rejected her Messiah, God sent the gospel to the Gentiles that they might be saved. This was predicted by Moses in Deuteronomy 32:21. Paul had mentioned this truth before in Romans 9:22–26. One reason why God sent the gospel to the Gentiles was that they might provoke the Jews to jealousy (Rom. 10:19; 11:11). It was an act of grace both to the Jews and to the Gentiles.
>
> —*Be Right*, page 130

9. How do you feel about God's sending of the gospel to the Gentiles as a means of provoking the Jews to jealousy? How is this an act of grace? What does this tell you about the "mysterious ways" God often works in order to enact His plan for the world?

From the Commentary

> God wants to use us to share the gospel with both Jews and Gentiles. God can use our feet and our arms just as He

used Paul's. Jesus Christ wept over Jerusalem and longed
to gather His people in His arms. Instead, those arms were
stretched out on a cross where He willingly died for Jews
and Gentiles alike. God is long-suffering and patient, "not
willing that any should perish, but that all should come to
repentance" (2 Peter 3:9).

—*Be Right*, page 131

10. What are some ways God can use our feet and arms to share the gospel
with Jews and Gentiles?

Looking Inward

Take a moment to reflect on all that you've explored thus far in this study
of Romans 10:1–21. Review your notes and answers and think about how
each of these things matters in your life today.

> *Tips for Small Groups: To get the most out of this section, form pairs
> or trios and have group members take turns answering these questions.
> Be honest and as open as you can in this discussion, but most of all, be
> encouraging and supportive of others. Be sensitive to those who are
> going through particularly difficult times and don't press for people to
> speak if they're uncomfortable doing so.*

11. Are you zealous about your faith? How do you show this in your daily

life? Does your zeal for traditions or activities ever outshine your zeal for God Himself? Why do you think this is, and what can you do about it?

12. If you've accepted Christ, how did that happen? Was it difficult or simple? In what ways do you make your approach to faith more difficult than it needs to be?

13. How are you sharing your faith today with others? What are some things you can do differently to make yourself more available to those who don't yet know Jesus as their Savior?

Going Forward

14. Think of one or two things that you have learned that you'd like to work on in the coming week. Remember that this is all about quality, not quantity. It's better to work on one specific area of life and do it well than to work on many and do poorly (or to be so overwhelmed that you simply don't try).

Do you need to let go of the law and embrace God's grace? Do you need to become more confident in sharing the gospel of Christ with others? Be specific. Go back through Romans 10:1–21 and put a star next to the phrase or verse that is most encouraging to you. Consider memorizing this verse.

Real-Life Application Ideas: Make a point this week to talk to at least one non-Christian friend about your faith. This should be someone you've already known as a friend, someone you've earned the right to talk to about spiritual things. Look for natural windows of opportunity in your conversations that will allow you to share your story without sounding as if you're forcing your beliefs on the person.

Seeking Help

15. Write a prayer below (or simply pray one in silence), inviting God to work on your mind and heart in those areas you've previously noted. Be honest about your desires and fears.

Notes for Small Groups:
- *Look for ways to put into practice the things you wrote in the "Going Forward" section in this lesson. Talk with other group members about your ideas and commit to being accountable to one another.*
- *During the coming week, ask the Holy Spirit to continue to reveal truth to you from what you've read and studied.*
- *Before you start the next lesson, read Romans 11:1–36. For more in-depth lesson preparation, read chapter 10, "God Is Not Through with Israel!" in* Be Right.

Not Done Yet!
(ROMANS 11:1–36)

Before you begin …
- *Pray for the Holy Spirit to reveal truth and wisdom as you go through this lesson.*
- *Read Romans 11:1–36. This lesson references chapter 10 in* Be Right. *It will be helpful for you to have your Bible and a copy of the commentary available as you work through this lesson.*

Getting Started

From the Commentary

> Paul devoted all of Romans 11 to presenting proof that God is not through with Israel. We must not apply this chapter to the church today, because Paul is discussing a literal future for a literal nation. He called five "witnesses" to prove there was a future in God's plan for the Jews.
>
> —*Be Right,* page 135

1. As you review Romans 11:1–36, who or what do you see as the "five witnesses" that prove there is a future for the Jews in God's plan?

More to Consider: Note that Paul's conversion is recorded three times in Acts (chapters 9, 22, and 26). Wiersbe suggests this is because the author of Acts, Luke, wanted to show Paul's conversion as an illustration of the future conversion of the nation Israel. Read 1 Timothy 1:16. How do Paul's words here support this idea?

2. Choose one verse or phrase from Romans 11:1–36 that stands out to you. This could be something you're intrigued by, something that makes you uncomfortable, something that puzzles you, something that resonates with you, or just something you want to examine further. Write that here. What strikes you about this verse?

Going Deeper

From the Commentary

The accounts of Paul's conversion tell very little that parallels our salvation experience today. Certainly none of us has seen Christ in glory or actually heard Him speak from heaven. We were neither blinded by the light of heaven nor thrown to the ground. In what way, then, is Paul's conversion "a pattern"? It is a picture of how the nation of Israel will be saved when Jesus Christ returns to establish His kingdom on earth.

—*Be Right*, page 136

3. Can you relate to Paul's story even though it might not mirror your own? Explain. What about his story is universally true about coming to Christ? If his story is a picture of how Israel will be saved, what do you think that means?

From the Commentary

The fact that most of the nation has rejected Christ is no proof that God has finished with His people.

—*Be Right*, page 136

4. Read 1 Kings 19. How is the remnant of believers in this story like or unlike the remnant Paul refers to in Romans 9:27? Why is it important to note that this remnant is saved by grace and not by works?

From Today's World

The concept of "grace" is rare in popular media, but when it does appear, it is often notable by contrast to the themes of "you get what you deserve," or even more common, revenge. Think of the top television shows and top movies playing at your local movie theater.

5. Where do you see the theme of grace in popular media? Why do you think this is such a rare theme in movies and TV? Can grace and redemption apart from a church setting help nonbelievers understand more about the Christian faith? How can Christians take advantage of popular media's take on grace in reaching out to others?

From the Commentary

> This is what happened to Israel: Their spiritual blessings should have led them to Christ, but instead they became a snare that kept them from Christ. Their very religious practices and observances became substitutes for the real experience of salvation.
>
> —*Be Right*, page 137

6. How did spiritual blessings become a snare for the Israelites? How does this happen today in the Christian church?

From the Commentary

> Paul stated that the Gentiles had a vital ministry to Israel.
> Today, the saved Gentiles provoke Israel "to jealousy" (see
> Rom. 10:19) because of the spiritual riches they have in
> Christ. Israel today is spiritually bankrupt, while Chris-
> tians have "all spiritual blessings" in Christ (Eph. 1:3).
> (If an unsaved Jew visited the average church service,
> would he be provoked to *jealousy* and wish he had what
> we have—or would he just be provoked?)
>
> —*Be Right*, pages 138–39

7. Why is Israel "spiritually bankrupt"? What are the blessings they're missing out on that Christians receive? What would unsaved Jews see if they
visited your church? How would they respond to the message and the people? What does this tell you about how your church is presenting the gospel
message?

From the Commentary

> God accepted the founder of the nation, Abraham, and
> in so doing set apart his descendants as well. God also
> accepted the other patriarchs, Isaac and Jacob, in spite

of their sins or failings. This means that God must accept the "rest of the lump"—the nation of Israel.

—*Be Right*, page 139

8. In what ways does God's acceptance of the "rest of the lump" impact your understanding of the Jews? Of God Himself? How are we like Isaac and Jacob and the "rest of the lump" even though we are saved by grace?

From the Commentary

What has happened to Israel is all a part of God's plan, and He knows what He is doing. The hardening (or blinding, Rom. 11:7) of Israel as a nation is neither total nor final: it is partial and temporary. How long will it last? "Until the fulness of the Gentiles be come in" (Rom. 11:25).

—*Be Right*, page 141

9. As you look at Paul's explanation of God's plan for the Israelites, what does this tell you about God? About the future of the Jewish people?

From the Commentary

> God's gifts to Israel, and God's calling of Israel, cannot be taken back or changed, or God would cease to be true to His own perfect nature. The fact that Israel may not enjoy her gifts, or live up to her privileges as an elect nation, does not affect this fact one bit. God will be consistent with Himself and true to His Word no matter what people may do.
>
> —*Be Right*, pages 142–43

10. Think about gifts you've given or received that were not used. How is that like or unlike what Wiersbe writes in the excerpt? Why is God's consistency so important to our faith?

Looking Inward

Take a moment to reflect on all that you've explored thus far in this study of Romans 11:1–36. Review your notes and answers and think about how each of these things matters in your life today.

Tips for Small Groups: To get the most out of this section, form pairs or trios and have group members take turns answering these questions. Be honest and as open as you can in this discussion, but most of all, be encouraging and supportive of others. Be sensitive to those who are going through particularly difficult times and don't press for people to speak if they're uncomfortable doing so.

11. What is your reaction to Paul's explanation of God's plan for the Israelites? How does this fit with your understanding of God's love? God's overall plan for the world? For your life? What implications does this have for how you relate to your Jewish friends or your overall perception of the Jewish faith?

12. What are some of the religious practices that might keep you from seeing God clearly? When are you most likely to slip into a works-based faith rather than trusting in God's grace?

13. Reread Romans 11:33–36. How does this passage speak to you? How does the truth of these verses affect the way you approach doubt or questions about God's overall plan for the world in general and for you in particular?

Going Forward

14. Think of one or two things that you have learned that you'd like to work on in the coming week. Remember that this is all about quality, not

quantity. It's better to work on one specific area of life and do it well than to work on many and do poorly (or to be so overwhelmed that you simply don't try).

Do you need to study more about God's plan for the Jews? Learn to trust God's plan even though you might not understand it? Be specific. Go back through Romans 11:1–36 and put a star next to the phrase or verse that is most encouraging to you. Consider memorizing this verse.

Real-Life Application Ideas: Do some research on Judaism, focusing specifically on the Jewish people's hope for a Messiah. As you study, pray for all your Jewish friends, asking God to speak to them with the truth of His Son's role in redeeming us from sin and to enlighten you about their role in God's overall plan of redemption. Strike up some conversations with your Jewish friends on spiritual matters. Be a neighbor to them.

Seeking Help

15. Write a prayer below (or simply pray one in silence), inviting God to work on your mind and heart in those areas you've previously noted. Be honest about your desires and fears.

Notes for Small Groups:

- *Look for ways to put into practice the things you wrote in the "Going Forward" section in this lesson. Talk with other group members about your ideas and commit to being accountable to one another.*

- *During the coming week, ask the Holy Spirit to continue to reveal truth to you from what you've read and studied.*

- *Before you start the next lesson, read Romans 12:1— 13:14. For more in-depth lesson preparation, read chapter 11, "Right Relationships Mean Right Living," in Be Right.*

Right Relationships

(ROMANS 12:1—13:14)

Before you begin ...
- *Pray for the Holy Spirit to reveal truth and wisdom as you go through this lesson.*
- *Read Romans 12:1—13:14. This lesson references chapter 11 in* Be Right. *It will be helpful for you to have your Bible and a copy of the commentary available as you work through this lesson.*

Getting Started

From the Commentary

In all of his letters, Paul concluded with a list of practical duties that were based on the doctrines he had discussed. In the Christian life, doctrine and duty always go together. What we believe helps to determine how we behave. It is not enough for us to understand Paul's doctrinal explanations. We must translate our *learning* into *living* and show by our daily lives that we trust God's Word.

—*Be Right,* page 147

1. How do "doctrine and duty" work together according to this section of Romans? How do you translate learning into living? What are some examples of this from your own life?

> *More to Consider: The key idea in this passage is "relationships." How does having a right relationship with God impact the way we relate to other people? What are some of the most important aspects of a "right relationship with God"?*

2. Choose one verse or phrase from Romans 12:1—13:14 that stands out to you. This could be something you're intrigued by, something that makes you uncomfortable, something that puzzles you, something that resonates with you, or just something you want to examine further. Write that here. What strikes you about this verse?

Going Deeper

From the Commentary

Before we trusted Christ, we used our bodies for sinful

pleasures and purposes, but now that we belong to Him, we want to use our bodies for His glory.

—*Be Right*, page 148

3. What are the "sinful pleasures and purposes" people seek apart from a relationship with God? Does the desire for those things change after we become Christians? Explain. What does it mean to offer your body to God as a "living sacrifice"?

From the Commentary

We surrender our wills to God through disciplined prayer. As we spend time in prayer, we surrender our will to God and pray, with the Lord, "Not my will, but thy will be done." We must pray about everything, and let God have His way in everything.

—*Be Right*, page 149

4. How does prayer help in the process of renewing your mind (as Paul writes about in 12:2)? Go through Romans 12 and 13 and underline everything that requires the "surrendering of our wills to God." Now review what you've underlined. What does this tell you about letting God have His way?

From Today's World

The pressures of the world weigh down on all of us daily. There is the pressure to perform, the pressure to succeed, the pressure to look your best, the pressure to have the best of everything. Take a closer look at how these pressures present themselves in the lives of Christians. Do they come from work? From family? From the media? They all have one common theme: The pressure is exerted from the outside in.

5. How do you respond to external pressures? According to Paul, what are some ways we can respond appropriately? What are the character traits that the Holy Spirit wants to light within us that can transform the way we think, react, and live?

From the Commentary

> Each believer has a gift (or gifts) to be used for the building up of the body and the perfecting of the other members of the body. In short, we belong to each other, we minister to each other, and we need each other.
>
> —*Be Right*, page 150

6. What are some of the gifts Paul references in Romans 12:3–8? How can each of these gifts build up the body of Christ? Explain why all of the gifts are important.

More to Consider: Wiersbe writes that some people belittle their gifts and don't use them, while others boast of gifts they don't have. Both of these responses are evidence of pride. How does pride negatively impact the body of Christ?

From the Commentary

> Spiritual gifts are tools to build with, not toys to play with or weapons to fight with.
>
> —*Be Right*, page 151

7. What are ways people might "play" or "toy" with their spiritual gifts? How do people use them as weapons? Describe what it looks like to "build" with your spiritual gifts.

From the Commentary

> Christian fellowship is much more than a pat on the back and a handshake. It means sharing the burdens and the blessings of others so that we all grow together and glorify the Lord. If Christians cannot get along with one another, how can they ever face their enemies?
>
> —*Be Right*, page 152

8. Describe some of the best examples of Christian fellowship you've witnessed or experienced. What are some of the characteristics of good fellowship? Circle words or phrases in this Scripture passage that exemplify what it means to enjoy fellowship.

More to Consider: Reread Romans 12:17–21. How easy or difficult is it for Christians to respond to their enemies in the ways Paul describes? Why is it so easy for us to want to retaliate when others wrong us? What role does the Holy Spirit play in changing our attitudes toward our enemies?

From the Commentary

God established human government because humankind is sinful and must have some kind of authority over us. God has given the sword to rulers, and with it the authority to punish and even to execute. Capital punishment was ordained in Genesis 9:5–6, and it has not been abolished. Even though we cannot always respect the person in office, we must respect the office, for government was ordained by God.

—*Be Right*, page 155

9. Consider the people who govern your life and the world around you. Which of Paul's words are most difficult to "swallow" in Romans 13:1–7? What are some of the things you appreciate about those who are in authority over you? Some things you don't agree with? How does your response to authority impact the way others view your faith?

From the Commentary

> "Love one another" is the basic principle of the Christian life. It is the "new commandment" that Christ gave to us (John 13:34). When we practice love, there is no need for any other laws, because love covers it all. If we love others, we will not sin against them.
>
> —*Be Right*, page 156

10. How might the governments and leaders who impact your world change if they were to embrace wholeheartedly the "love one another" principle? What would that look like in practical terms?

Looking Inward

Take a moment to reflect on all that you've explored thus far in this study of Romans 12:1—13:14. Review your notes and answers and think about how each of these things matters in your life today.

Tips for Small Groups: To get the most out of this section, form pairs or trios and have group members take turns answering these questions. Be honest and as open as you can in this discussion, but most of all, be encouraging and supportive of others. Be sensitive to those who are going through particularly difficult times and don't press for people to speak if they're uncomfortable doing so.

11. What are some of the ways you're currently offering your body to God as a living sacrifice? What are some of the challenges you face as you attempt to do this? How will you respond to those challenges?

12. What are some ways you devote yourself to others? How do you show sincere love to family members, friends, coworkers, and strangers?

13. How well do you express love to those people whom you consider enemies? How well do you submit to authorities (even if you don't agree with them)? If you're struggling with either of these things, what steps can you take to be more loving? More appropriately submissive to leaders?

Going Forward

14. Think of one or two things that you have learned that you'd like to work on in the coming week. Remember that this is all about quality, not quantity. It's better to work on one specific area of life and do it well than to work on many and do poorly (or to be so overwhelmed that you simply don't try).

Do you need to learn how to be a living sacrifice? Discover how to love those you disagree with? Submit to authority? Be specific. Go back through Romans 12:1—13:14 and put a star next to the phrase or verse that is most encouraging to you. Consider memorizing this verse.

Real-Life Application Ideas: Choose to work on one of the following two challenges Paul presents in this Romans passage: (1) loving your enemies, or (2) submitting to authority. Think about a specific person you're having a difficult time loving or a specific leader you're having a difficult time respecting, then list two or three things you can do to change your attitude so it matches what Paul is teaching. (The leader doesn't have to be a political one; we have leaders in every area of our lives.) Consider talking with a close friend about your ideas so he or she can be an advocate and an accountability partner.

Seeking Help

15. Write a prayer below (or simply pray one in silence), inviting God to work on your mind and heart in those areas you've previously noted. Be honest about your desires and fears.

Notes for Small Groups:
- *Look for ways to put into practice the things you wrote in the "Going Forward" section in this lesson. Talk with other group members about your ideas and commit to being accountable to one another.*
- *During the coming week, ask the Holy Spirit to continue to reveal truth to you from what you've read and studied.*
- *Before you start the next lesson, read Romans 14:1—16:27. For more in-depth lesson preparation, read chapters 12 and 13, "When Christians Disagree" and "Man on the Move," in* Be Right.

We Just Disagree
(ROMANS 14:1—16:27)

Before you begin ...
- *Pray for the Holy Spirit to reveal truth and wisdom as you go through this lesson.*
- *Read Romans 14:1—16:27. This lesson references chapters 12 and 13 in* Be Right. *It will be helpful for you to have your Bible and a copy of the commentary available as you work through this lesson.*

Getting Started

From the Commentary

Disunity has always been a major problem with God's people. Even the Old Testament records the civil wars and family fights among the people of Israel, and almost every local church mentioned in the New Testament had divisions to contend with.

—*Be Right,* page 161

1. List a few examples of disagreements you've witnessed in your church experience. What is usually at the source of the division?

More to Consider: Often the most bitter disputes in churches and other organizations are prompted by silly little things—things that really don't matter in the larger scheme. What are examples of these "things that don't matter"? What are the kinds of things that are worthy of discussion and disagreement?

2. Choose one verse or phrase from Romans 14:1—16:27 that stands out to you. This could be something you're intrigued by, something that makes you uncomfortable, something that puzzles you, something that resonates with you, or just something you want to examine further. Write that here. What strikes you about this verse?

Going Deeper

From the Commentary

> It is encouraging to know that our success in the Christian
> life does not depend on the opinions or attitudes of other

Christians. God is the Judge, and He is able to make us
stand.

—*Be Right*, pages 163–64

3. In what ways do Christians base their success on the opinions and attitudes
of others? Why is this so tempting? How can we live as Paul admonishes and
look only to God for our significance or measure of success?

From the Commentary

Knowledge plus love helps the weak person grow strong.
—*Be Right*, page 167

4. According to Paul, how do we live out this "knowledge plus love" truth?
Underline key truths in Romans 14:1—16:27 that speak to this idea.

From Today's World

Though the basic tenets of the Christian faith have not changed since the
days of the early church, certainly the church itself has changed, marching
forward (sometimes a step or two behind) along with our culture. This has

prompted plenty of disagreements in the church on everything from the relative amorality of something we take for granted today like radio (people once feared radio because Satan was the "prince of the power of the air") to the more controversial topics like secular movies or music or even that old standby: dancing.

5. What happens if the church doesn't keep up with the culture? What are the best ways to assure the church is relevant without becoming worldly? Why do some of these issues of cultural relevancy cause division in the church?

From the Commentary

> There are certain truths that all Christians must accept because they are the foundation for the faith. But areas of honest disagreement must not be made a test of fellowship. If you have a sincere conviction from God about a matter, keep it to yourself and do not try to force everybody else to accept it.
>
> —*Be Right*, page 169

6. Make a list of some of these truths "all Christians must accept." How

does this list compare with what your church teaches? What are some of the things that tend to divide people in your church? Now list a few convictions that aren't in that "all Christians must accept" list. How do Christians live out these convictions without causing division?

More to Consider: Respond to this quote from Wiersbe: "A person's spiritual maturity is revealed by his discernment."

From the Commentary

> Disunity and disagreement do not glorify God; they rob Him of glory. Abraham's words to Lot are applicable to today: "Let there be no strife, I pray thee, between me and thee ... for we be brethren" (Gen. 13:8).
>
> —*Be Right*, page 171

7. Read Romans 15:1–7 again. Circle any reference to "others" in this passage. What is the main theme of these verses? How can unity positively impact the body of Christ? How can we develop unity without losing the uniqueness and individuality we've been given by God?

From the Commentary

> The supreme example of ministry must always be Jesus
> Christ. "But I am among you as he that serveth" (Luke
> 22:27). He came first of all to minister to the Jews, that
> through Israel He might be able to minister to the Gen-
> tiles. "To the Jew first" is a principle that was followed in
> the earthly ministry of Christ and in the early ministry of
> the church.
>
> —*Be Right*, page 175

8. What does Romans 15:7–8 tell us about how we're to minister to others? Paul writes about how we're to be like Christ, but then describes some
ways he does this himself in his own ministry to the Jews. Circle those places
in Romans 15:14–22 where Paul tells how Christ has shown him how to
minister.

From the Commentary

> The Holy Spirit empowered Paul to minister, and enabled
> him to perform mighty signs and wonders. The miracles
> God gave Paul to do were "signs" in that they came from
> God and revealed Him to others. And they were "won-
> ders" in that they aroused the wonder of the people. But

their purpose was always to open the way for the preaching of the gospel.

—*Be Right*, pages 178–79

9. Why do you think there are fewer "signs and wonders" in today's church? What is a good test of whether or not a sign or wonder is truly something from God? What are other ways we are to open the way for the preaching of the gospel?

From the Commentary

In [Romans 16] Paul greeted at least twenty-six people by name, as well as two unnamed saints, and he also greeted several churches that were meeting in homes. He closed with greetings from nine believers who were with him in Corinth when he wrote the letter.

—*Be Right*, page 181

10. What is the significance of all of these greetings at the end of Paul's letter? What sort of greeting might Paul have given people in your church had he spent time there? In what ways can you seek to enlarge your own personal network of Christ-followers?

Looking Inward

Take a moment to reflect on all that you've explored thus far in this study of Romans 14:1—16:27. Review your notes and answers and think about how each of these things matters in your life today.

Tips for Small Groups: To get the most out of this section, form pairs or trios and have group members take turns answering these questions. Be honest and as open as you can in this discussion, but most of all, be encouraging and supportive of others. Be sensitive to those who are going through particularly difficult times and don't press for people to speak if they're uncomfortable doing so.

11. Have you ever been involved in a disagreement or division in your church? If so, what was the cause of the problem? How did you respond to it? What did you learn in that situation that can help you avoid division or disagreements in the future?

12. What are some of the personal convictions about faith that could potentially cause division among others in your church or faith community? How well are you doing at keeping these convictions from causing division? How do you respond when others speak their minds about issues you think are not universal truths "all Christians must accept"?

13. What sort of greeting might Paul have given you had he spent time with you in the past year? What sort of greeting would you want him to offer? What changes can you make today to become the type of person who might receive such a greeting in the future?

Going Forward

14. Think of one or two things that you have learned that you'd like to work on in the coming week. Remember that this is all about quality, not quantity. It's better to work on one specific area of life and do it well than to work on many and do poorly (or to be so overwhelmed that you simply don't try).

Do you need to avoid holding tight to issues that cause division? Do you need to learn how to build unity? Be specific. Go back through Romans 14:1—16:27 and put a star next to the phrase or verse that is most encouraging to you. Consider memorizing this verse.

Real-Life Application Ideas: As a way to celebrate the many people in your church who have made a positive difference in your life and the lives of others, write a "greetings and commendations" letter like the one Paul uses to close Romans. Make a point to talk to each of these people in the coming week.

Seeking Help

15. Write a prayer below (or simply pray one in silence), inviting God to work on your mind and heart in those areas you've previously noted. Be honest about your desires and fears.

Notes for Small Groups:
- *Look for ways to put into practice the things you wrote in the "Going Forward" section in this lesson. Talk with other group members about your ideas and commit to being accountable to one another.*
- *During the coming week, ask the Holy Spirit to continue to reveal truth to you from what you've read and studied.*

Summary and Review

Notes for Small Groups: This session is a summary and review of this study. Because of that, it is shorter than the previous lessons. If you are using this in a small-group setting, consider combining this lesson with a time of fellowship or a shared meal.

Before you begin ...
- *Pray for the Holy Spirit to reveal truth and wisdom as you go through this lesson.*
- *Briefly review the notes you made in the previous sessions. You'll be referring to previous sections throughout this bonus lesson.*

Looking Back

1. Over the past twelve lessons, you've examined Paul's letter to the Romans. What expectations did you bring to this study? In what ways were those expectations met?

2. What is the most significant personal discovery you've made from this study of Romans?

3. What surprised you most about Paul's explanation of the role of the Israelites in God's greater plan? What, if anything, troubled you?

Progress Report

4. Take a few moments to review the "Going Forward" sections of the previous lessons. How would you rate your progress for each of the things you chose to work on? What adjustments, if any, do you need to make to continue on the path toward spiritual maturity?

5. In what ways have you grown closer to Christ during this study? Take a moment to celebrate those things. Then think of areas where you feel you still need to grow and note those here. Make plans to revisit this study in a few weeks to review your growing faith.

Things to Pray About

6. Romans is a book rich with theology. As you reflect on the words Paul has written, ask God to reveal to you those truths that you most need to hear. Revisit the book often and seek the Holy Spirit's guidance to gain a better understanding of what it means to be righteous before God.

7. The messages in Romans cover a wide variety of topics, including grace and the law; the universality of the message to all people; and lots of advice on how to get along with others. Spend time praying on each of these topics.

8. Whether you've been studying this in a small group or on your own, there are many other Christians working through the very same issues you discovered when examining Paul's letter to the Romans. Take time to pray for each of them, that God would reveal truth, that the Holy Spirit would guide you, and that each person might grow in spiritual maturity according to God's will.

A Blessing of Encouragement

Studying the Bible is one of the best ways to learn how to be more like Christ. Thanks for taking this step. In closing, let this blessing precede you and follow you into the next week while you continue to marinate in God's Word:

May God light your path to greater understanding as you review the truths found in the book of Romans and consider how they can help you grow closer to Christ.

More great Wiersbe BE Books for your library.

With over 4 million volumes in print, these timeless books have provided invaluable insight into the history, meaning, and context of virtually every book in the Bible.

BE Right
Warren W. Wiersbe
978-1-4347-6847-6

BE RIGHT
Explore the topics of salvation, justification, and the righteousness of God through the commentary of Romans, Paul's "how-to-manual" for disciples.

To learn more visit our Web site or locate a Christian bookstore near you.

The "BE" series . . .

For years pastors and lay leaders have embraced Warren W. Wiersbe's very accessible commentary of the Bible through the individual "BE" series. Through the work of Cook International, the "BE" series is part of a library of books made available to indigenous Christian workers. These are men and women who are called by God to grow the kingdom through their work with the local church worldwide. Here are a few of their remarks as to how Dr. Wiersbe's writings have benefited their ministry.

"Most Christian books I see are priced too high for me . . .
I received a collection that included 12 Wiersbe
commentaries a few months ago and I have
read every one of them.
I use them for my personal devotions every day and they
are incredibly helpful for preparing sermons.
The contribution Cook International is making to the
church in India is amazing."

—Pastor E. M. Abraham, Hyderabad, India